THE SPIDER MOON

KATE BROWN

David Fickling Books
OXFORD · NEW YORK

THE SPIDER MOON

A DAVID FICKLING BOOK 978 0 385 61827 4

First published thanks to the amazing DFC weekly comic,
May 2008 – March 2009 (Come back soon!!)

This edition published in Great Britain in 2010 by David Fickling Books,
a division of Random House Children's Books
A Random House Group Company

1 3 5 7 9 10 8 6 4 2

DAVID FICKLING BOOKS
31 Beaumont Street, Oxford, OX1 2NP

www.kidsatrandomhouse.co.uk
www.rbooks.co.uk

Addresses for companies within The Random House Group Limited
can be found at: www.randomhouse.co.uk/offices.htm

THE RANDOM HOUSE GROUP Limited Reg. No. 954009

A CIP catalogue record for this book is available
from the British Library.

Printed and bound in China

For all readers of The DFC, everywhere!

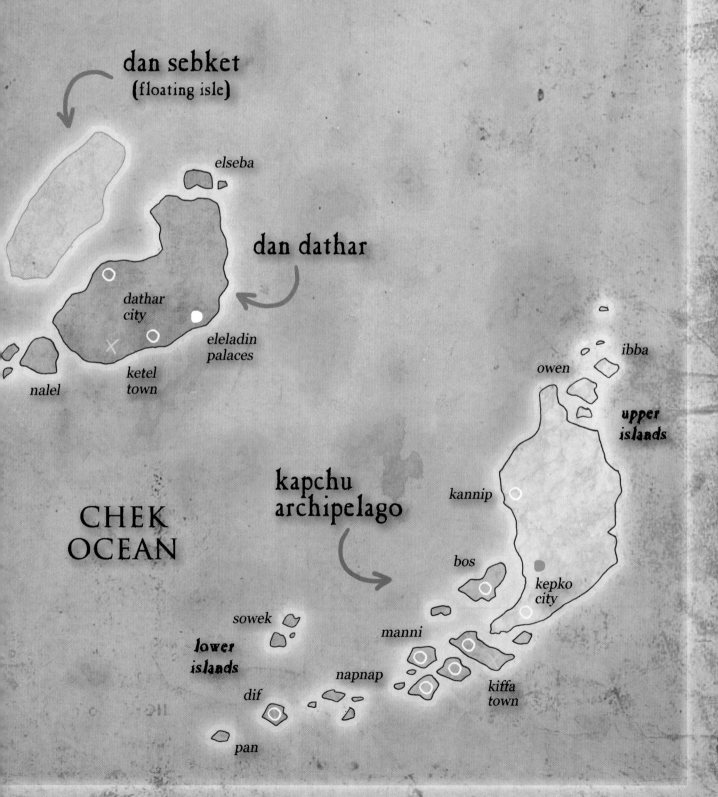

ENTOPA
OCEAN

N

dan sebket
(floating isle)

elseba

dan dathar

dathar
city

eleladin
palaces

ketel
town

nalel

CHEK
OCEAN

kapchu
archipelago

owen

ibba

upper
islands

kannip

bos

kepko
city

sowek

lower
islands

manni

dif

napnap

kiffa
town

pan

IN THE FAR NORTH, THERE ARE ANCIENT CAVES, WITH MURALS PAINTED BY LONG-DEAD HANDS...

THEY TELL A PROPHECY OF OUR HOMELANDS BEING CRUSHED BY THE FALLING SKY.

THAT FATE HAS BEEN A SHADOW OVER OUR PEOPLE EVER SINCE.

O ESCAPE, SOME TRIED
OSSING THE MOUNTAINS
TO THE WEST, TO
UNCHARTED PARTS
OF THIS WORLD.

OTHERS SAILED TOWARDS
THE RISING SUN IN THE EAST.

NONE RETURNED.

TIME PASSED, AND WE WAITED
FOR THE SIGNS TO COME.

THEN, A YEAR AGO, THE STARS BEGAN TO FALL. JUST LIKE THE MURALS SHOW.

THE END HAS BEGUN ... IN MY LIFETIME.

THE SPIDER MOON

WELL! I'M NOT GONNA LET THEM STOP ME, SO —

BEKKA!

AH! YEAH! I'M COMING!

BEKKA, KAY'S WAITING OUTSIDE.

I KNOW, MUM!

NO, NO, NO!

MUM! THERE'S NO NEED!

I'M REALLY *REALLY* NEARLY READY!

I'LL GO AND TELL HER YOU'RE COMING, THEN.

TODAY IS MY DIVING EXAM!

MY DIVING "SISTER" IS K —

BEKKA!

...KAY LAU.

(NNF!)

I'VE BEEN TRAINING WITH HER FOR WEEKS AND WEEKS!

TODAY IS MY ONE CHANCE TO PROVE I CAN BE A GREAT DIVER!

IF I MESS UP, I'LL NEVER GET TO DIVE AGAIN. THAT'S THE RULES.

BUT, I WON'T MESS UP! I CAN DEFINITELY, *DEFINITELY* DO THIS!

I'LL BE A GREAT DIVER. I'VE GOT TO... TO HELP US ALL SURVIVE...

15

OUR PEOPLE ARE BORN WITH WEBBED HANDS... WE HAVE BIGGER LUNGS, TOO!

SO IF I KEEP UP MY TRAINING...

EVENTUALLY I'LL B
ABLE TO DIVE FO
ALMOST TWO HOU

...HM...

... SHOULDN'T I BE ABLE TO SEE THE BOTTOM BY NOW ..?

...K...?

...KKA...!

BEKKA...?!

...YES...?

...OH!

KAY...!

ARE YOU ALRIGHT?!

I DIVED AFTER YOU, BUT I COULDN'T SEE YOU ANYWHERE!

I CAME ASHORE, AND YOU WERE HERE...

BEKKA, YOU'RE *COMPLETELY* DRY!

WHAT HAPPENED?!

UM...

UM, I GOT THE SAND, KAY.

W-WELL DONE.

I DON'T KNOW HOW YOU DID IT, BUT... I'LL PASS YOU.

YOU CAN DIVE WITH THE REST OF US.

I THINK THE OCEAN...

OR SOMETHING, AT LEAST...

FAVOURS YOU, BEKKA.

EVER SINCE I PASSED MY DIVING TEST...

...I'VE BEEN SAILING OUT WITH KAY AND ALL THE CANOES EVERY MORNING!

I HELPED BUILD THIS ONE! AND I PAINTED IT A NAME, TOO.

(...THOUGH KAY SAID IT WON'T *ACTUALLY* MAKE IT GO FASTER...)

NOW MY BEST DIVE TIME IS FORTY-FIVE MINUTES. KAY'S IS ONE-HUNDRED AND FIFTEEN...!

SO I'VE STILL GOT TO STAY QUITE CLOSE TO HER...

ESPECIALLY AFTER THE, UM...PROBLEMS...I HAD WITH MY EXAM...

(ACTUALLY, I THINK SHE'S MORE NERVOUS THAN ME!)

(...AND, UM...)

(...I NEVER TOLD HER ABOUT THE WHALE.)

ALSO! I'VE DISCOVERED THAT FII, MY DODECAPOD...

MAKES A GREAT DIVING PARTNER...

... 'CAUSE HE HEADS STRAIGHT FOR *THESE* PRICKLY THINGS!

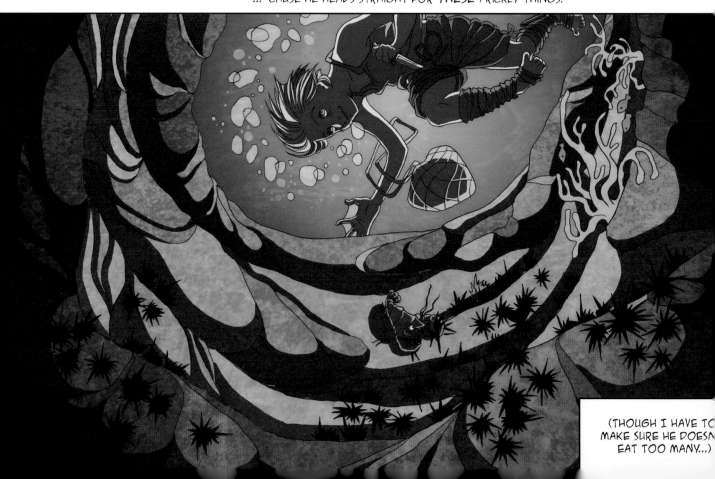

(THOUGH I HAVE TO MAKE SURE HE DOESN EAT TOO MANY...)

THESE THINGS ARE CALLED SPINEFISH! THEY'RE OUR MAIN TRADE.

EVERY DAY WE SEND OUR CATCHES OFF TO BE MADE INTO OIL FOR FUEL.

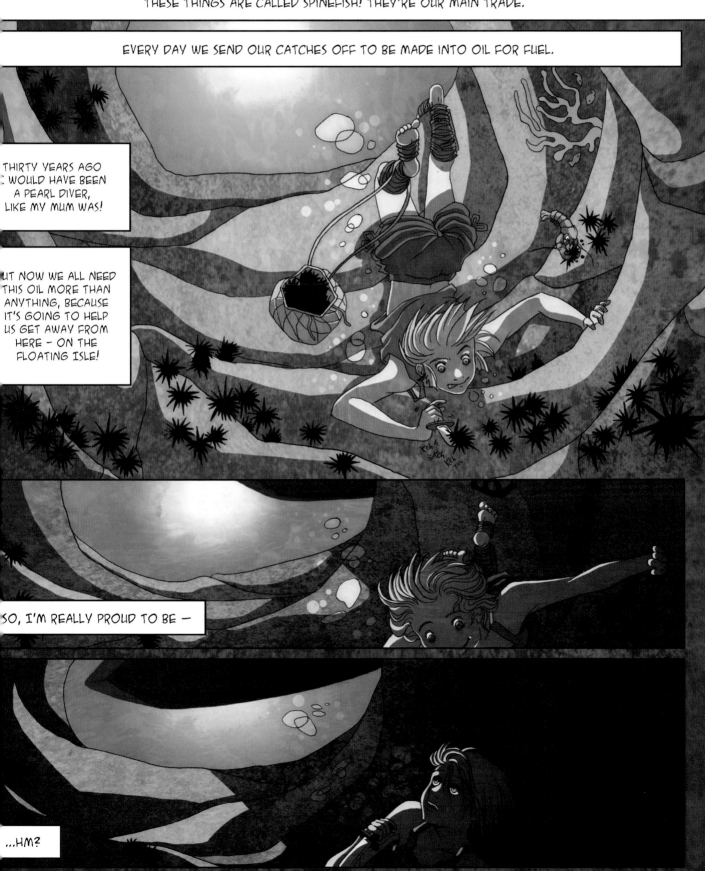

THIRTY YEARS AGO
I WOULD HAVE BEEN
A PEARL DIVER,
LIKE MY MUM WAS!

BUT NOW WE ALL NEED
THIS OIL MORE THAN
ANYTHING, BECAUSE
IT'S GOING TO HELP
US GET AWAY FROM
HERE – ON THE
FLOATING ISLE!

SO, I'M REALLY PROUD TO BE –

...HM?

26

WHAT'S HAPPENED?

KAY, YOUR MOTHER WAS —

CHAIRMAN EKLI LAU WAS *ARRESTED.*

THUD

ME AND MY BROTHER SAW A WHOLE LOAD OF THE BIRD-FOLK...

...STORM INTO THE MIDDLE OF EKLI'S COUNCIL MEETING AND BUNDLE EVERY SINGLE MEMBER INTO THAT BOAT!

THE BIRD-FOLK CAME *HERE* ...?

part two

41

part three

PARDON FOR THE INTRUSION.
I HOPE YOU RESTED WELL.
NO.
CHAIRMAN EKLI HAS REQUESTED THAT HER DAUGHTER JOIN HER AT THE MEETING.
OH!
YES, OF COURSE.
WAIT, NO!
WHAT ABOUT ME? I WANT TO TELL THEM WE'RE STILL SENDING THE FISH TO THE REFINERY, AND –
BEKKA – IT'S ALRIGHT. WE'LL BE FINISHED QUICKLY AND THEN WE CAN GO HOME, OKAY?
HEY! THIS IS JUST AS MUCH MY PROBLEM AS –

60

TCH.

ALRIGHT.

ALRIGHT, IF THAT'S WHAT IT TAKES TO MAKE YOU STAY *QUIET*, I'LL TAKE YOU TO THE MEETING.

AND YES, I AM "*SNEAKING*."

...IF YOU HAVE TO PUT IT THAT WAY.

SO *NO*, I DON'T WANT THE GUARDS NOTICING.

THANK YOU.

I'M ON MY WAY TO DO SOMETHING.

AND I'LL DO THAT *FIRST*...

THEN I'LL TAKE YOU WHERE YOU WANT...

... IS THAT FINE WITH YOU?

UH.

Y-YEAH, THAT'S FINE.

UM...

PIT-PAT PIT-PAT PIT-PAT

H-HEY... YOU'LL GET INTO A LOT OF TROUBLE FOR THIS, WON'T YOU...?

WELL —

WON'T THEY FIND OUT YOU'VE BEEN VISITING YOUR SISTER, AND EVERYTHING?

... BLAH BLAH AND ABSOLUTELY **MAY** NOT TAKE THE BLAH BLAH ...

W-WELL... MAYBE I'VE CAUSED ENOUGH TROUBLE FOR —

HEY!

(LOOK, IF YOU'RE QUIET, WE DON'T EVEN HAVE TO OPEN THE DOOR...)

KRII...

HA!

(HEY, YOU REALLY **ARE** GOOD AT SNEAKING, AREN'T YOU!)

NUDGE! NUDGE!

BUT THE FUEL ISN'T HERE, COUNCILLOR LAU!
THE OIL REFINERIES ARE TELLING US YOUR COMMUNITY IS REFUSING TO CO-OPERATE!
WHO SHOULD WE BELIEVE?
LOOK: I CAN'T SPEAK FOR THE REFINERIES.
ALL I KNOW IS THAT MY PEOPLE ARE STILL SHIPPING THE SPINE-FISH TO THEM!
WHATEVER THE PROBLEM IS, THE REFINERIES HAVE NOT SAID A WORD TO US.
IF THEY REALLY HAVE STOPPED TRADING TO YOU...
WELL, I DON'T KNOW WHAT THEY THINK THEY'RE DOING.
THEY'RE LYING IS WHAT THEY'RE DOING!
(KAY'S RIGHT! THEY REALLY ARE LYING!)
(BUT —)
(LOOK! LOOK, THESE ARE FROM YESTERDAY!)
(WE SHOULD SHOW THEM!)
(THIS COULD BE EVIDENCE!)
(YEAH!)

TO BE CONTINUED...

Kapchu

The Kapchu Archipelago is divided into two halves: the Upper Islands and the Lower Islands. The Lower towns and villages are populated almost exclusively by native Kapchu folk, as people from other countries find living on the smaller isles rather tough. The Upper towns and cities have a wide mix of people. Kepko City, in particular, is considered quite a fashionable place to live.

Kapchu islanders have unique physical characteristics, the most immediately obvious being their hair colour, ranging from blue to green. More subtle are their webbed fingers, which allows for comfortable swimming in their warm seas. The country's main exports are salt, flax & flowers, and – in more recent years – oil. The people tend to wear bright colours, and their diets are mostly fish, seaweeds, steamed foods, etc.

Dathar

People from the surrounding countries perceive the "Bird-folk" of Dathar to be haughty and aloof. In reality, they are simply a rather self-contained race of people, with gentle dispositions and a love of music and the arts.

Their most striking feature is the small, ornamental wings that emerge as Dathar children reach the age of approximately 13. They vary subtly in colour, and are mostly dusky greys, browns and blues. Their main exports are rare spices, and the highly sought-after deep blue cloth, made from a type of flower that only grows near the Dathar coasts. The people follow vegetarian diets, consisting mainly of vegetables, spices and pulses. They are also the only state to have a ruling monarchy.

Pallakachin

Pallakachin is the largest continent, with vast distances between each major town or city, typically linked with a scattering of smaller villages or hamlets. The climate of Pallakachin is a fair bit cooler than in other countries, and it frequently snows in the most northern areas.

In general, the people are rather calm and sturdy, and do not fluster easily. Their houses are built from local stone, and their exports include metals, stone and livestock. Their clothes are mainly of dyed wool and linen, and their diets consist of dried meats, stews and root vegetables.

Bekka Kiski

Bekka lives in Kiffa Town, on the Lower Islands of the Kapchu archipelago. She is intensely energetic and can't abide feeling useless, and is likely to act first and think later. Her energy comes from not wishing to waste a moment after growing up in an environment in which the world is expected to collapse.

Bekka is extremely fond of Kapchu home-cooking, and her favourite meal is scrambled Groxhen eggs with Gailak leaves and shrimp sauce. In fact, she eats anything and everything as often as she can, though defends this by explaining she burns it all off when swimming.

Bekka and Fii met one day when Bekka was out collecting shells from a rock-pool and discovered the lone Dodecapod snoozing on a rock. She decided to become friends with him, and so took him home and put him in a box. Initially, Fii made many escape attempts, but has since realised the error of his ways, discovering that if he hangs around Bekka he will get to eat as many Spinefish as he can possibly manage. Bekka sewed a pocket to her trousers for him to ride in, as he is not a very fast walker on land. Dodecapoda are terrestrial creatures, though need to remain damp. Their defence mechanism is to play dead. In general, they are not considered to be very good pets.

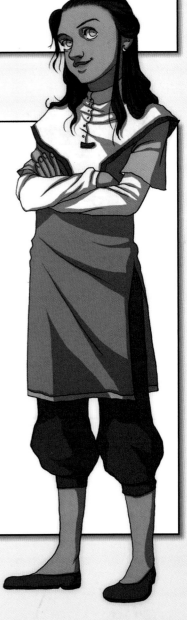

Prince Kaliel sebneth-Eleladin

Kaliel is second-in-line to the Dathar throne, after his sister. In general he is calm and polite, although his temperament sometimes veers towards being overly serious, which sometimes causes him to act rather haughtily. As rumours began circulating that his sister might never recover, and Kaliel began to realise that he could be the next King, he took it upon himself to try his best at everything, and to treat everyone fairly, in order to assure his parents that he could be a good successor. Sometimes he can take this too far, and end up compromising himself by trying to assert justice.

After Sera became confined to bed, and Kaliel had no-one of his own age to play with, he took up a new hobby of becoming acquainted with all of the secret passages and spy-holes in the palaces in order to eavesdrop all important meetings that occur, particularly those surrounding the Skyship, which he holds great faith in.

Kaliel has a severe weakness for dairy-products and desserts, most especially chocolate. Sometimes his sneaking abilities are channelled into "testing" food from the Palace kitchens. So far, he has not been caught.

making a cover image
from start to finish

For this image, I designed three or four rough "covers" in Photoshop that I loosely coloured, to give an impression of how the final illustration might look. The image we chose to take forward in the end was this picture of Bekka swimming with some fish.

After this, I began drawing the under-sketch. I worked on A3 80gsm plain paper with an HB 0.5 clicky pencil. A3 is my favourite size to work on! I also drink a lot of tea at this stage... The Spider Moon was powered by tea!

Then, I traced a neat pencil line over the rough pencil onto a new sheet of paper, using a light-box to let me see the rough lines clearly through the new sheet. That's the line-work done! I then scanned my lines into Photoshop at 600dpi, and cleaned up any smudges or mistakes. I also tinted the lines to a greenish-blue so they would match the finished colours a little better.

Colouring is my favourite stage! I really enjoy it. First, I began by laying down the flat colours. I usually make separate layers for the character, and for the background or other major elements, underneath the line-work layer. After this, I applied shading to Bekka on a new layer, set to Multiply.

Because I find simple flat colours look a little synthetic against the pencil line that I use, I usually apply a texture layer over the top of my illustrations. Here, I overlaid photographs of water-ripples, and mottled textures for the fish-scales. Playing about with this technique can create interesting effects. I also added gradients to the shading, and to the fish, to stop the colours from looking too flat.

Effects like the light shining through the water are added last. These were created by drawing strokes of blues and cyans, blurring them a bit and setting the layer-mode to overlay, then putting them over the top of the entire image. I also added shadows cast by Bekka and the fish. Finally, the title was applied, and then it was done! Phew!

More stories from

 **Library**

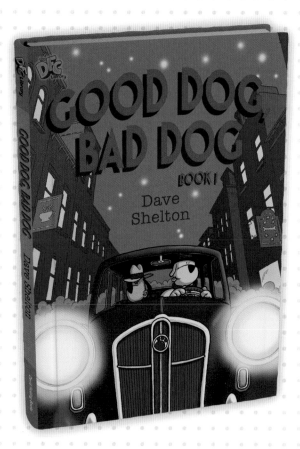

MEZOLITH:

A magical story of ten-thousand-year-old myth and legend. A young boy named Poika will battle fear and hardship for the good of his tribe.

GOOD DOG, BAD DOG:

Canine crooks will have to watch their tails as doggy detectives, Bergman and McBoo, sniff out crime.

Collect them all!